In honor of my great-grandfather, Charles Adelbert
Steinert—immigrant, Union soldier and bugler,
blacksmith, farmer, and justice of the peace—who
loved his new country and was willing to fight for it
— RS

To Gio, for helping me on my journey
— NHA

Thank you to Nick Adams, Director of Transgender
Representation, and Rich Ferraro, COO at GLAAD,
for their thoughtful and enthusiastic collaboration
in helping us tell Albert's story.

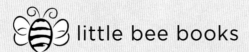 little bee books

251 Park Avenue South, New York, NY 10010
Text copyright © 2020 by Rob Sanders
Illustrations copyright © 2020 by Nabigal-Nayagam Haider Ali
Photo credit: page 40, bottom right: © Kimberly M Knight
All rights reserved, including the right of reproduction in whole or in part in any form.
Manufactured in China LEO 0520
First Edition
10 9 8 7 6 5 4 3 2 1
Library of Congress Cataloging-in-Publication Data is available upon request.
ISBN 978-1-4998-0936-7
littlebeebooks.com

For more information about special discounts on bulk purchases,
please contact Little Bee Books at sales@littlebeebooks.com.

THE FIGHTING INFANTRYMAN

★ ★

The Story of Albert D. J. Cashier, Transgender Civil War Soldier

Written By
Rob Sanders

Illustrated By
Nabi H. Ali

★ FOREWORD ★

More and more gender-diverse children are growing up in supportive environments than ever before. Families, schools, religions, and sports organizations are all trying to make more room for children who do not easily fit within gender stereotypes. At the same time, other gender-creative young people are still met with denial, hostility, bullying, and suppression. In either of these environments and all of those in between, a transgender child may be the only person like them in their whole circle. At best, they will know only a handful of other kids whose gender is atypical, and probably no adults who are like them. Surveys tell us that trans people make up about 1 to 2 out of every 100 people in the US. While that may be more than most people would think, it can still be a very lonely place to be when you are a young child who feels like there is no one else like you.

These youngsters, and all of the people who know and love them, need to know that they are not alone, that they are part of a long and noble history of gender-diverse people who have contributed to society in important ways. Trans and other gender-diverse kids need to be able to see themselves in stories about real people who have had the courage to live as their authentic selves throughout history and across the cultures of the world. This is something in short supply for gender-diverse children who are so often isolated from others like themselves, and frequently bullied for their difference.

The Fighting Infantryman, about the life of Civil War soldier Albert D. J. Cashier, is a sweetly told true story about the life of a trans man who served his country nobly. It does not shy away from the difficulties of being trans in the midnineteenth century. It forthrightly portrays the isolation that was the price Albert paid through most of his life to keep private the fact that he was assigned female at birth. When, in his elder years, Albert became ill and his gender history was revealed, officials questioned whether he was really the man known as Albert D. J. Cashier. They sought to cancel his soldier's pension, and he was subjected to unwanted sensationalist publicity and forced to wear women's clothing. Happily, the story ends with redemption. Albert's former comrades in arms came forward to defend the man by whose side they fought, and forced the government to continue his pension and, upon his death, give him a proper military funeral and burial. Despite his travails, and because of his bravery and the loyalty it inspired in the soldiers who fought by his side, Albert D. J. Cashier is remembered as a man who fought selflessly for his country.

—Aaron Devor, PhD, Chair in Transgender Studies, University of Victoria, Canada

Jennie Hodgers collected seashells along the windy shores of Clogherhead, County Louth, Ireland.

She tended sheep in the fields.
The work was easier in boys' clothes.

Sometime later, she and her
stepfather sailed to America
as stowaways.
Jennie dressed as a boy.
It was more practical—
and safer—that way.

When the two of them arrived in
New York City, they needed money.
Jennie found work in a shoe factory.
It was a job for a boy.
Jennie fit right in.

The winds of history blew through America.
The winds of change were whirling around Jennie Hodgers, too.
Jennie moved west.

By the time she arrived in Belvidere, Illinois, and started working as a farmhand, Jennie had a new name and a new identity . . .

Albert D. J. Cashier.

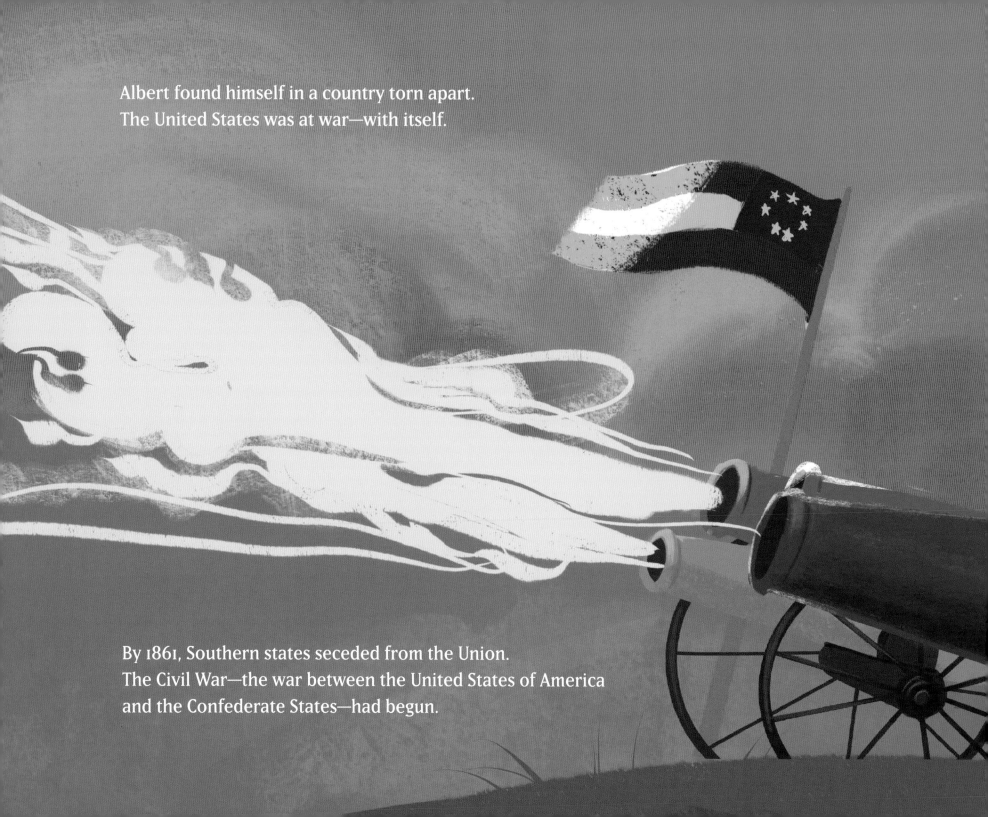

Albert found himself in a country torn apart.
The United States was at war—with itself.

By 1861, Southern states seceded from the Union.
The Civil War—the war between the United States of America
and the Confederate States—had begun.

The winds of war raged through the country.
In the summer of 1862, President Abraham Lincoln called for
more volunteers to fight—hundreds of thousands of volunteers.

On August 6, 1862, like most other men in Boone County, Illinois,
Albert was ready to enlist in the Union Army.

He was nineteen years old.
It wouldn't be easy.
It wouldn't be safe.
But Albert made a choice.

He answered questions in his thick Irish brogue.
He signed his name with an X.
But there was more to enlisting than signing your name.
Each volunteer had to pass a physical examination.

Albert was five feet, three inches tall.
Maybe his height wouldn't matter.

He was one of the smallest volunteers.
Maybe his size wouldn't matter.

He was strong and healthy.
Maybe, just maybe, that's all that *would* matter.

One by one, the doctor examined each recruit.
Albert waited.
And waited.
His heart thumped beneath his shirt.

Finally, it was Albert's turn.
The doctor closely examined Albert's
small hands and feet.
That was all he needed to see.

Albert passed the physical.
He could breathe easy.
He could relax.
He could be himself . . . for now.

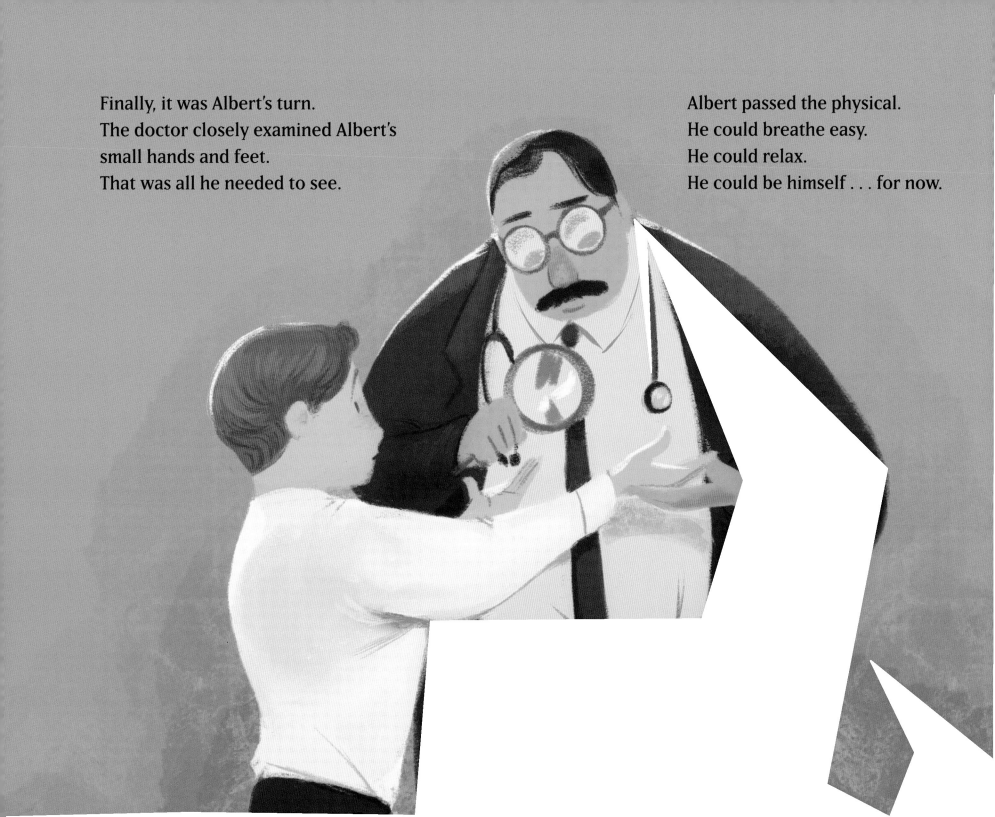

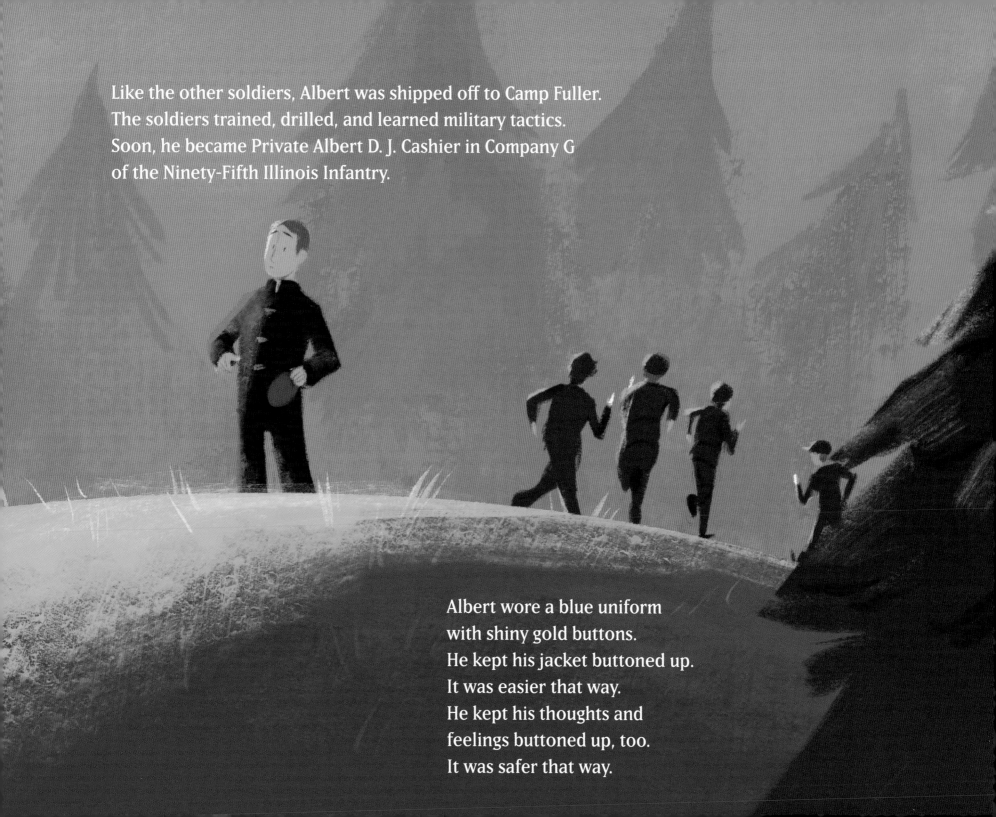

Like the other soldiers, Albert was shipped off to Camp Fuller.
The soldiers trained, drilled, and learned military tactics.
Soon, he became Private Albert D. J. Cashier in Company G
of the Ninety-Fifth Illinois Infantry.

Albert wore a blue uniform
with shiny gold buttons.
He kept his jacket buttoned up.
It was easier that way.
He kept his thoughts and
feelings buttoned up, too.
It was safer that way.

Albert was like every other soldier.
He worked hard.
He answered the bugle's morning call.
He toted heavy supplies.
This was the choice he made.

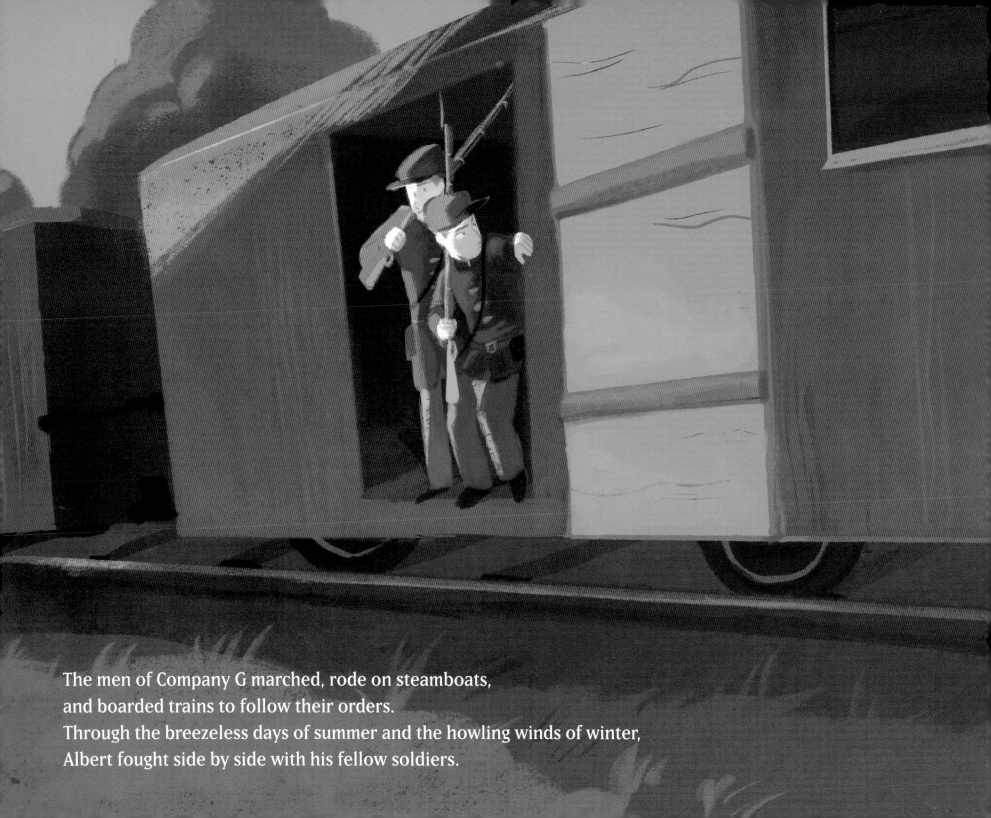

The men of Company G marched, rode on steamboats,
and boarded trains to follow their orders.
Through the breezeless days of summer and the howling winds of winter,
Albert fought side by side with his fellow soldiers.

In Kentucky, Tennessee, and Mississippi.
Through woods, streams, and fields.

From Memphis to Vicksburg to Natchez.
Across rivers and swamps.

The Battle of Bayou. The Red River expedition.
The Battle at Guntown. The Battle of Nashville.

Winter. Spring. Summer. Fall.
Into Arkansas and Missouri and back to Tennessee.
Albert was there for every step, every day, every month, every year.

During one battle, when the United States flag fell, Albert grabbed the stars and stripes and climbed a tree while bullets whizzed around him.
He hung the flag, and it flew proudly once again.

Many soldiers were wounded. Others were killed. Albert and his fellow Union soldiers continued to serve their country and they continued to fight.

On April 9, 1865, the Civil War finally came to an end.
The bloodiest four years in American history were over.
A breeze of peace began to flow through the country.

Albert and the others in the Ninety-Fifth headed back to Illinois.
They mustered out of the Union Army on August 17, 1865.

The United States of America had changed forever.
So had Albert.
Had it been easy?
Had it been safe?

No. Not for a country trying to be
what it was meant to be.
No. Not for a man trying to be
who he was meant to be.

After the war, Albert traveled
through Illinois, settling in Saunemin.
He continued to live as a man.
His identity fit him as snug as his suspenders.

Albert couldn't read or write, but he could work.

And he did—he grew plants in a nursery business,
farmed, and worked as a handyman.

He lit the town's kerosene streetlamps each
evening and extinguished them each morning.

Like other veterans, he was paid a military pension.

The small pension and what he earned from
odd jobs was all the money Albert had.

But he also had pride. He was proud
of being a Civil War veteran.

Some remembered Albert voting in every election.
They recalled him wearing his blue uniform on Memorial Day.
They reminisced about him leading children to lay flowers on
the graves of fallen soldiers.

Some boys in town teased Albert.
"Drummer boy," they called after him.
"I was a fighting infantryman," he bellowed at the boys.

For decades, Albert lived his life quietly, with few friends.

In 1911, when Albert was in his sixties, everything changed. His leg was broken in an automobile accident.

A doctor, Albert's employer, and two friends
suddenly learned he wasn't born a man.
Albert asked them not to tell anyone.
They agreed.

Albert could breathe easy.
He could relax.
He could continue being himself . . . for now.

On May 5, 1911, as Albert's health worsened, he was admitted to the Illinois Soldiers' and Sailors' Home. The doctors and nurses there also learned that Albert wasn't born a man. Albert begged them not to tell anyone. They agreed—at least for a while.

But all too soon, someone spoke to a reporter.

Then another reporter heard the news.
And another. And another.
Soon, newspapers in Albert's town, his state,
and throughout the country shouted:

Pensioned
Civil War Soldier
is a Woman

SERVED IN WAR
AS A BOY

WOMAN FOUGHT
IN THE CIVIL WAR

Albert had no idea the story
of his life had become big news.
No one told him.
Newspapers were hidden from him.
The news was kept a secret.

When the United States government caught wind of the story,
they started asking questions:
Who is this person?
Why is a woman receiving a military pension?
Could this possibly be the same person who served in the Civil War?

Men from Company G visited the hospital.
They saw the old man in the faded blue uniform.
They talked to him.
Soon, they were talking to doctors, reporters, and government officials.
"This *is* Albert D. J. Cashier," they said.

Albert's health grew worse.
In 1913, he was sent to a different hospital,
and the doctors there saw things differently.
To them, Albert was a woman.

It didn't matter that he had served in the Civil War.
It didn't matter that he had lived his life as a man.

Albert was sent to the women's section of the hospital.
He was required to wear skirts and dresses.
He wasn't given a choice.

Albert had no idea that his army comrades
were fighting a new battle. A battle for him.
They testified on his behalf.
They wrote letters.

They fought for Albert to be treated with respect and to receive his pension.
Then, on February 10, 1915, the army declared:

The evidence in this case...shows beyond any doubt
that the pensioner is the person who rendered the
service...Identity may be accepted.

Finally, Albert and his soldier comrades could breathe easy.
They could relax.
The government agreed—Albert *was* who he always said he was.

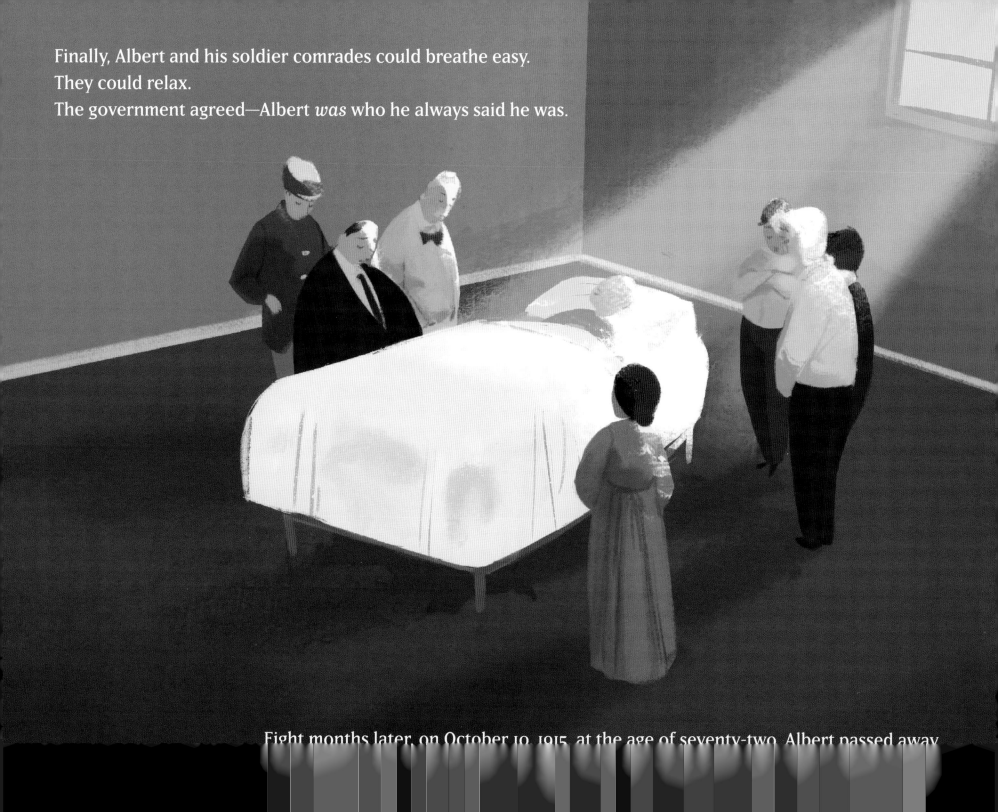

Eight months later, on October 10, 1915, at the age of seventy-two, Albert passed away.

Albert's fellow soldiers made sure the story of Albert D. J. Cashier did not blow away with the winds of history. His service to his country would not be a secret.

The men of the Ninety-Fifth Illinois Infantry insisted that Albert be given
a military funeral—just like every other man who'd served in the Union Army.
Albert's body was dressed in his blue uniform with shiny gold buttons.
The American flag was draped over his coffin.
Nurses from the hospital sang.

Albert was buried in the Sunny Slope Cemetery in Saunemin, Illinois.

His tombstone was inscribed:

ALBERT D J CASHIER

CO G
95 ILL INF

1843
1915

Life had not been easy for Albert.
Life had not always been safe.

But the proud Civil War veteran lived life the best way he could.
It was more than a choice—it was who Albert D. J. Cashier was.

★ AUTHOR'S NOTE ★

The story of an illiterate immigrant who became a soldier in the Civil War could have been lost forever. If it had not been for the accident that caused Albert's broken leg, he might not have ended up in the hospital. And if he had not been in the hospital, others might not have learned of his story.

The accident, Albert's hospitalization, and newspaper articles that were later published caused the Interior Department of the United States government to conduct a formal investigation of Albert D. J. Cashier. Could it be true that the elderly person dressed in a faded Civil War uniform sitting in the Soldiers' and Sailors' Home in Quincy, Illinois, could have fought in the Civil War? Or was the person drawing the war pension in the name of Albert D. J. Cashier an impostor, a woman pretending to be him? People who knew Albert stepped up to say he was who he said he was. Fellow soldiers and old friends testified about what they knew of the man.

The depositions these people gave became part of Albert's pension file. The file is a 192-page collection of papers that is housed today in the National Archives. These papers—depositions, letters, medical records, forms, bank documents, and interviews from some of Albert's friends and comrades—serve as the record of his life.

In many of the depositions, people testified about what Albert told them. Some members of the staff of the Soldiers' and Sailors' Home used what they learned from Albert to help locate additional information about his family in Ireland. Some of the things Albert said were contradictory. Some things were false. Since dementia had set in, perhaps his mind wasn't clear and sharp.

It is believed that Albert was born on Christmas Day in 1843 and that his mother was not married when he and his twin brother were born. Albert said that he collected seashells at the shore, that he wore boys' clothing while tending sheep, and that he dressed as a boy to sail to America as a stowaway with his stepfather. Albert took the last name of his stepfather. He reported that his stepfather found work in a shoe factory in New York City and got Albert a job there. The job was for a boy. Albert fit right in.

Albert said he ended up in Illinois, continued to live as a man, and worked as a farmhand. He said that he signed up for the Union Army for excitement. There is no doubt that he served in the army for nearly three years, traveled 9,960 miles, and participated in forty battles and skirmishes.

★ WHAT FRIENDS AND COMRADES SAID ABOUT ALBERT ★

The following are excerpts from depositions taken during the United States Interior Department investigation regarding Albert's status as a veteran. The investigation was launched to determine if Albert was who he said he was, and if he were entitled to continue to receive a military pension.

Albert's friends and army comrades wrestled with his gender during their depositions. They had always known Albert as a man but had learned he was not born male. Some referred to Albert using the pronoun *he*, others used *she*, and a few even mixed the two pronouns. In the end, the investigation proved that Albert was who he said he was and that he was entitled to his pension. Albert died eight months after the investigation concluded.

"I marched day after day with him for the first eight months. . . . He was one of the smallest men in the company and had very small hands. He seemed to be able to do as much work as anyone in the company. . . . While I was in the service I never suspicioned that he was not a man, and I never heard any talk to that effect." —Mr. Joy Saxton, Belvidere, Illinois, private in Company G

"The firt [sic] I ever knew Albert D. J. Cashier, was when he joined Co G 95 ILL Inf. . . . I was well acquainted with Cashier while he was in the service and would see him every day. . . . I saw in the paper where his sex had been discovered and I wanted to go to Quincy to see if it was the real Cashier. I went for that purpose. . . . When I first saw her I recognized her at once as being the Albert D. J. Cashier who served in Co. G." —Mr. Robert Horan, Belvidere, Illinois, corporal in Company G

"While he was in the service I did not dream that he was a woman but we used to talk about him not having a beard. I never heard any talk in the army about him not being a man." —Mr. Eli Brainard, Belvidere, Illinois, private in Company G

"I remember Albert D. J. Cashier distinctly. He was a short well built man and a brave little soldier." —Mr. Robert D. Hannah, Huron, South Dakota, corporal in Company G

"I have known Albert Cashier some 44 or 45 years. That is about the time he came to my father's place in the country. He made our home his home. . . . In the course of nursing Albert I discovered that the sex was that of a female. He asked me then not to tell any one that he was a woman." —Mrs. Nettie Rose, Pontiac, Illinois, friend

"The first I remember Albert Cashier was when he came to my parents about 45 years ago. . . . For years he herded cattle on the prairie for my father. . . . I have visited him twice since he has been in the Soldier's Home in Quinacy [sic], and I know that the man or woman who is there, under the charge of Mr. Scott, is the identical Albert D. J. Cashier who lived with us and whom I have known about 45 years." —Miss Anah Chesbro, Pontiac, Illinois, friend

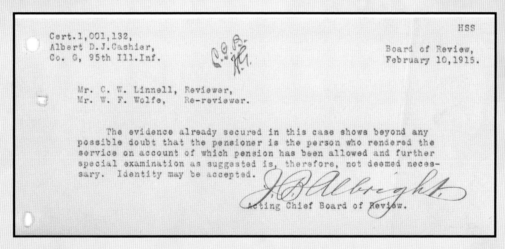

The document above is from the "Approved Pension File for Albert D. J. Cashier, Company G, Ninety-Fifth Illinois Infantry Regiment (XC-2573248)," page 171. The document reads:

"The evidence already secured in this case shows beyond any possible doubt that the pensioner [Albert D. J. Cashier] is the person who rendered the service [in the Civil War] on account of which pension has been allowed and further special examination as suggested is, therefore, not deemed necessary. Identity may be accepted."

J.B. Albright
Acting Chief Board of Review

★ ALBERT'S MOTIVATION ★

We don't know for certain why Albert D. J. Cashier lived his life as a man. Maybe doing so was more comfortable, more convenient, or safer. Maybe Albert lived as a man because it provided him with more opportunities and choices in life. But it's likely that Albert was transgender and identified as a man. Today, transgender people look up to Albert D. J. Cashier as a man who lived his truth the way he saw fit.

★ TRANSGENDER PEOPLE IN HISTORY ★

Transgender people have always existed in every culture and country on earth. *Transgender* is when a person looks like a boy or a girl when they're born, but inside they know that their gender is different from what is written on their birth certificate. Before the 1900s, there wasn't one word that everyone used to describe that experience. In Native American tribes, Hawaii, and other countries, different terms were used: words such as *nadleehi*, and *mahu, hijra*, and *fa'afafine*. So, when we remember people who lived as the opposite gender in the past, while we can't say for certain they were transgender, it is certainly possible they were—even though they would not have known that term.

★ GLOSSARY ★

brogue [brohg] *noun*—an Irish accent
dementia [dih-**men**-sh*uh*] *noun*—a loss of mental ability and memory
enlist [en-list] *verb*—to volunteer for military service
identity [ahy-**den**-ti-tee] *noun*—the condition of being oneself
mustered out [**muhs**-ter-deh **out**] *verb*—to be discharged from military service
pension [**pen**-shuhn] *noun*—a set amount of money paid to former soldiers in recognition of their service

recruits [ri-**kroots**] *noun*—newly enlisted members of the armed forces
secede [si-**seed**] *verb*—to leave or withdraw from a country or other body
skirmish [**skur**-mish] *noun*—a fight between small groups of soldiers
stowaway [**stoh**-uh-way] *noun*—a person who hides aboard a ship for free transportation
veterans [**vet**-er-uhns] *noun*—persons who served in the military

SOURCES

Primary Sources
"Albert D. J. Cashier," *The Dispatch*, Moline, Illinois, page 7: October 13, 1915.

Approved Pension File for Private Albert D. J. Cashier, Company G, 95th Illinois Infantry Regiment (XC-2573248), National Archives Catalog, https://catalog.archives.gov/id/36605129.

"Case of Famous Woman Soldier Again in Limelight: Albert D. [sic] Cashier, Once Inmate of Soldiers' Home at Quincy Wants Increase Pension," *Moberly Weekly Monitor*, Moberly, Missouri, page 2: February 23, 1915.

"Cashier's Mystery of Soldiering Given to the World," *Belvidere Daily Republican*, Belvidere, Illinois, page 3: May 5, 1913.

The Civil War Day by Day: An Almanac 1861–1865 by E. B. Long with Barbara Long. Doubleday, Garden City, New York: 1971.

"Harrison Aldridge Acquainted with the 'Woman of Mystery,'" *The Decatur Herald*, Decatur, Illinois, page 13: June 1, 1913.

A History of the Ninety-fifth Regiment, Illinois Infantry Volunteers: From Its Organization in the Fall of 1862, Until Its Final Discharge from the United States Service, in 1865 by Wales W. Wood. Tribune Company's Book and Job Printing Office, Chicago: 1865.

Illinois Civil War Detail Report: Cashire [sic], Albert D J, Illinois State Archives.

Interview with C. W. Ives, *Omaha Bee*, Omaha, Nebraska: May 30, 1923.

"The Little Soldier of the 95th: Albert D. J. Cashier" by Gerhard P. Clausius. *Journal of the Illinois State Historical Society (1908–1984)*, Vol. 51, No. 4 (Winter, 1958), pages 380–387.

"Pensioned Civil War Soldier is a Woman," *St. Louis Post-Dispatch*, St. Louis, Missouri, page 61: May 25, 1913.

"Served in War As a Boy," *The Boyden Reporter*, Boyden, Iowa, page 1: December 2, 1915.

"Woman Fought in Civil War: Took Part in Forty Battles, According to Records," *The Canton Independent-Sentinel*. Canton, Pennsylvania, page 2: May 22, 1913. (Note: This article appeared in numerous papers.)

Secondary Sources
"Private Albert Cashier as Regarded by His/Her Comrades" by Rodney O. Davis. *Illinois Historical Journal*, Vol. 82, No. 2 (Summer, 1989), pages 108–112.

Information About Gender Identity
Who Are You? The Kid's Guide to Gender Identity by Brook Pessin-Whedbee. Jessica Kingsley Publishers, London: 2016.

The Gender Identity Workbook for Kids: A Guide to Exploring Who You Are by Kelly Storck, LCSW. New Harbinger Publications, Oakland: 2018.

★ TIMELINE ★

December 25, 1843

Jennie Hodgers is born in Clogherhead, Ireland

December 20, 1860– February 1, 1861

Seven southern states secede from the Union; The Confederate States of America is formed with Jefferson Davis as president

April 12–13, 1861

The bombardment of Fort Sumter, South Carolina, begins the Civil War

September 4, 1862

Albert's Ninety-Fifth Illinois Infantry musters into the Union Army

July 4, 1863

The Ninety-Fifth enters and takes possession of Vicksburg, Mississippi

May 18, 1864

The Ninety-Fifth fights in the Battle of Yellow Bayou

November 6, 1860

Abraham Lincoln is elected president and Hannibal Hamlin, vice president

March 4, 1861

Abraham Lincoln is inaugurated as president of the United States

August 6, 1862

Albert D. J. Cashier enlists in the Union Army

January 1, 1863

Lincoln issues the Emancipation Proclamation, freeing enslaved people

November 19, 1863

Lincoln delivers the Gettysburg Address

June 10, 1864

The Ninety-Fifth fights fiercely near Guntown, Mississippi